KEEPING MINIBEASTS

BEE

98

© 1989 Franklin Watts

First published in Great Britain in 1989 by
Franklin Watts
12a Golden Square
London W1

First published in the USA by
Franklin Watts Inc.
387 Park Avenue South
New York, NY. 10016

First published in Australia by
Franklin Watts Australia
14 Mars Road, Lane Cove
New South Wales 2066

UK ISBN: 0 86313 845 4
US ISBN: 0-531-10718-3
Library of Congress Catalog
Card No: 88-29669

Design: Edward Kinsey
Consultant: Michael Chinery

Printed in Italy by G. Canale & C S.p.A. - Turin

ISBN 0–531–15619–2 (pbk.)
First Paperback Edition 1991

KEEPING MINIBEASTS

BEETLES

TEXT AND PHOTOGRAPHS: BARRIE WATTS

CONTENTS

FRANKLIN WATTS

LONDON • NEW YORK • SYDNEY • TORONTO

What are beetles?

Beetles are found in all shapes and sizes.
Most of them can fly but keep their wings
under their wing cases when they are not
being used.

Some kinds of beetle live on the ground or even under water, whereas others, like ladybugs, climb plants to look for food.

Habitats

Beetles live in all kinds of habitats. They live in forests, in freshwater ponds and streams, houses and gardens. In the home, carpet beetles can cause damage to carpets and fabrics.

However, many beetles do good, especially those that feed on pests such as aphids. Some even feed on flower pollen and in doing so pollenate the flowers so that they can bear fruit.

You can collect beetles in any small plastic or cardboard box. Put only one beetle in each box because some beetles could easily fight. Some even eat each other.

The best time to look for beetles is on a sunny day. Flying beetles will be looking for food and can easily be found. Look under stones and rocks and you could find ground beetles.

A good way to collect ground living beetles is to make a pitfall trap. You can set the trap in a wood or even in a garden. All you need is a jar or a plastic cup, four stones and a small piece of wood.

Bury the cup level with the surface and cover it with the wood and stones. Compare beetles caught at different times of the day.

Put some food in the cup and see what attracts certain species. Always remove the traps when you have finished.

Handling

Beetles are easy to handle. Use a small paintbrush and a paper cup with the smaller ones because you can damage them if you pick them up in your hand.

Larger ones can be picked up but always be gentle. Do not worry if they give off a smelly fluid. This is their protection against predators.

An old aquarium with a net cover is the best container to keep beetles in. Ground beetles need a layer of earth in the bottom as well as pieces of wood and stones under which to hide.

The lid must have plenty of holes and the earth must be damp or the beetles will dry up. Make sure you put in a good supply of food.
If you are keeping more than one beetle, make sure they are the same type, so they do not eat each other. A shady windowsill is the ideal place to put your beetle home.

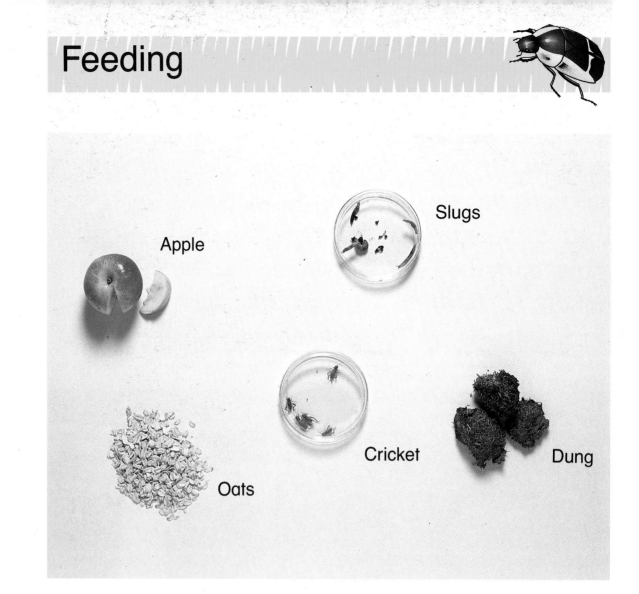

Apple

Slugs

Oats

Cricket

Dung

If the beetles are to stay healthy you must provide the right food for them. Sometimes it is difficult to know what they eat so watch them carefully before you collect them.

Ladybugs will eat aphids and dung beetles will eat horse manure. Black ground beetles are generally carnivorous and eat slugs and worms. You can also give them small pieces of meat.

Useful beetles

Some beetles are a great help in controlling pests in gardens and on farms. Ladybugs and their larvae eat a large number of aphids. A ladybug larva eats up to thirty aphids a day.

Dung beetles help to get rid of animal dung.
Some roll the manure into balls and bury it.
Then they lay their eggs in it so that the larvae
will have a ready supply of food when they
hatch.

Life-cycle

It is easy to study the life-cycle of a beetle.
Buy some mealworms from a pet shop and
put them in an old plastic container with holes
in the lid. Give them some dry bran and oats
to feed on and then leave them.

From time to time check to see how they are growing and put more food in if it is needed. Eventually you will see the mealworms, which are larvae, turn into pupae and finally into the adult beetles.

After the mealworm beetle has emerged from its pupa it is a light brown color, but will get darker as it gets older. The female will lay her eggs on the food. The eggs are like dust and almost too small to see.

When the eggs hatch, the larvae that emerge are what we call the mealworms. They are very small, just like cotton threads. They soon get bigger and need to change their skin just like a caterpillar. When they get to 30mm (1 ¼in) long they are ready to turn into pupae.

When you have finished studying the beetles always return them to the same habitat. Do not release any foreign beetles or ones that are likely to become pests, such as the mealworm beetles.

If your garden has too many aphids in it, add some ladybugs to eat them. If you have too many slugs, release some ground beetles. They will eat them every night — it is much better than using chemicals.

Unusual facts

The heaviest insect in the world is the Goliath Beetle from Africa, it weighs 100g (4oz).

The oldest beetle was found in Southend-on-Sea in Essex, England. It was a Splendor Beetle and it had spent 47 years as a larva.

The smallest insects in the world are the Hairywinged Beetles. They are only 0.2mm long and weigh only 0.005mg.

The glow-worm is a beetle. The wingless female uses the light in its tail to attract male beetles so that they can mate.

Index